*In starting and waging a war, it is not right that matters, but victory.*

—Adolf Hitler, 1939

# WORLD WAR II
## The Axis

When Germany invaded Poland on September 1, 1939, it confirmed what many countries feared. Adolf Hitler and his armies had begun an aggressive campaign to expand German control. The world war that followed would last six years and cost over 70 million lives.

World War II: The Axis focuses on the major Axis powers—Germany, Italy, and Japan—and on Hitler's rise to power. It also looks at dictatorships as a form of government.

**A-1**

# CONTENTS

# On the Brink of War

After losing World War I (1914–1918), Germany was forced to sign a peace agreement. This agreement was called the "Treaty of Versailles." The treaty forced Germany to give up land and weapons. It also forced Germany to make war **reparations**. Germany was not happy with the conditions of the treaty.

Other treaties had been signed after World War I as well. Both Italy and Japan signed peace agreements that they didn't like. They felt they had been cheated. Adding to this pressure was the worldwide business slump known as the Great Depression (1929–1939).

A number of forceful leaders rose to power during this time. By 1936, the Soviet Union, Germany, Japan, and Italy had become **dictatorships**. Their dictators wanted to expand their rule. They did so by invading weaker countries. By 1939, the world was once again on the brink of war.

Adolf Hitler stands before the Eiffel Tower in Paris, France, in 1940 (left).

# World War II Time Line

| | |
|---|---|
| January 30, 1933 | Adolf Hitler is appointed chancellor of Germany. |
| September 1, 1939 | Germany invades Poland—World War II begins. |
| September 3, 1939 | Britain, Australia, New Zealand, and France declare war on Germany. |
| September 5, 1939 | The United States declares its neutrality. |
| September 10, 1939 | Canada declares war on Germany. |
| May–June 1940 | French defenses collapse—British troops evacuate from Dunkirk. |
| June 10, 1940 | Italy declares war on France and Great Britain. |
| July–October 1940 | Germany attempts to defeat Great Britain's Royal Air Force in the Battle of Britain. |
| September 27, 1940 | Germany, Italy, and Japan sign a pact, forming the Axis Powers. |
| March 1941 | Congress passes the *Lend-Lease Act*. |
| June 1941 | German troops invade the Soviet Union. |
| December 7–8, 1941 | Japan bombs American military bases at Pearl Harbor in Hawaii. The United States, Britain, and Canada declare war on Japan. |
| March 1942 | The U.S. government begins moving Japanese Americans to relocation camps. |
| June 1942 | U.S. planes sink four Japanese aircraft carriers in the Battle of Midway. |
| July 1943 | The government of Italian dictator Benito Mussolini is overthrown. |
| June 6, 1944 | D-Day—Allied troops, led by General Eisenhower, land on the beaches of Normandy, France, as part of "Operation Overlord." |
| April 30, 1945 | Hitler kills himself as Soviet troops approach his quarters in Berlin. |
| May 7, 1945 | Germany surrenders in Reims, France. |
| August 6, 1945 | The United States drops an atomic bomb on Hiroshima, Japan. |
| August 9, 1945 | An atomic bomb is dropped on Nagasaki, Japan. |
| September 2, 1945 | Japan officially surrenders, ending World War II. |

**reparations**
: payment for damages

**dictatorships**
: systems of government in which rulers have total power over their countries

A-3

# Hitler: Total Power

## 1919–1939

Like many Germans, Adolf Hitler believed that his country had been badly treated after World War I. In 1919, Hitler joined the German Workers' Party. A year later, Hitler was elected the party's leader. The party became known as the **Nazi** Party. It used **racism** and intimidation to gain power. Many Germans disagreed with Nazi beliefs.

Hitler promised to turn the economy around. He said he would make Germany a military superpower again. He also promised to take back the land Germany had lost. Many Germans began to support Hitler. His speeches and writings contained lies and direct attacks against Jewish people and other groups. Still, many Germans took pride in Hitler's extreme form of **nationalism**.

In 1933, Hitler became the leader of Germany. Soon he took on the role of dictator, a leader who has total power. Over the next six years, Hitler worked at forming a new Germany.

Hitler's goal was to expand German land and build a new **empire**. However, foreign leaders continued to hope that Hitler's plans would not lead to war. Then, on September 1, 1939, Germany invaded Poland. World War II had begun.

When Hitler invaded other countries, he demanded complete obedience from the people. This woman in Czechoslovakia is saluting Hitler against her wishes (right).

The German government salutes Hitler in March 1938 after Germany successfully took over Austria.

CASE STUDY

# Mein Kampf ("My Struggle")

In November 1923, Hitler tried to overthrow the German state of Bavaria. More than 2,000 members of Hitler's private army marched against the Bavarian government. The plot failed, and Hitler was sentenced to five years in prison.

While in prison, Hitler began writing a book called *Mein Kampf* about his life and his beliefs (right). The book blamed the Jewish people for all the world's problems. Hitler was supposed to serve five years, but he was released from prison after only nine months. *Mein Kampf* went on to become the basis for Hitler's rise to power—about 10 million copies had been sold by the end of the war.

# The Axis: Italy

## 1935–1943

In the years leading up to World War II, several dictators rose to power—Hitler in Germany, Benito Mussolini in Italy, and Emperor Hirohito in Japan. These leaders had a major influence on world politics. They began aggressive campaigns to increase their countries' territories. They wanted to build huge empires.

Mussolini used violence to take control of Italy. His goal was to make Italy a world power through **fascism**. He believed in the idea that nation and race were more important than individuals.

In 1935, Italy invaded the African country of Ethiopia. By May 1936, the Italians had overpowered Ethiopia's army. The aggressive nations of Germany and Italy agreed to support one another. In 1936, they joined together to form the **Axis Powers**. Japan joined them in 1940.

Mussolini was a great supporter of Hitler. He publicly agreed with the Nazi leader on all things. Privately, however, Mussolini disagreed with some of Hitler's actions. This photo of the two leaders driving through a German crowd, Mussolini (left) and Hitler (right), was taken in Munich, in 1940.

# The World during World War II

**fascism**
> a political movement that supports an all-powerful government

**Axis Powers**
> refers to the union formed among Germany, Italy, and Japan between 1939 and 1945

**Allies**
> Great Britain, France, the Soviet Union, the United States, Canada, Australia, and New Zealand

**Key**

- Allies before Pearl Harbor
- Allies after Pearl Harbor
- Axis Powers
- Changed from Axis to Allies
- Neutral

## PROFILE

# Benito Mussolini 1883–1945

Italian dictator Benito Mussolini (right) ruled Italy as head of the Fascist Party between 1922 and 1943. His party took control of education and business in Italy, and they also controlled the newspapers and radio stations.

Like Hitler, Mussolini dreamed of creating an empire. However, the Italian Army often needed help from the German Army. After the **Allies** defeated the German and Italian forces in North Africa, Mussolini was arrested. A new leader of Italy was appointed in 1943.

# The Axis: Japan

Japan was the third major member of the Axis. It entered the war in 1941. Since the mid-1930s, Japan had been waging a brutal war against China. The United States wanted to stop Japan's expansion into Southeast Asia. It blocked oil supplies and trade to Japan. The Japanese responded by bombing the U.S. naval base at Pearl Harbor in Hawaii on December 7, 1941. Canada, Great Britain, and the United States declared war on Japan on December 8.

Hitler viewed Japan's attack on Pearl Harbor as an unexpected advantage. He believed that Japan's attack might keep the United States out of the war in Europe. This would allow him to continue to expand German territory. To show support for what Japan had done, he ordered both Germany and Italy to declare war on the United States, too.

The attack on Pearl Harbor was initially a great success for Japan. Most of the U.S. Navy's ships and aircraft had been destroyed. However, the attack would eventually prove to be a mistake for Japan.

The raid on Pearl Harbor was unexpected (left). Japan had kept the plan a secret even from Germany.

General Hideki Tojo (right) was appointed prime minister of Japan in October 1941. Tojo was quick to join the war after trade talks with the United States broke down. Tojo was forced to resign from his position after a series of military failures in July 1944.

"**N**ow it is impossible for us to lose the war! We now have an ally who has never been [defeated] in 3,000 years!"

—*Adolf Hitler, on hearing about the Japanese attack on Pearl Harbor*

## CASE STUDY

# Japanese Americans

After the bombing of Pearl Harbor, many Americans began to distrust Japanese Americans. In 1942, the U.S. government moved about 110,000 Japanese Americans into relocation camps (above and right). Once there, they were not allowed to leave. About two-thirds of the people moved into camps were U.S. citizens, but they were not treated as such. These Japanese Americans lost their jobs and their homes. The imprisonment of Japanese Americans is an example of wartime discrimination. Still, many Japanese Americans joined the war effort and fought to defend the United States.

# Nazi Propaganda

Joseph Goebbels was one of Hitler's most loyal followers. He was in charge of Nazi **propaganda**. This included newspapers, speeches, and posters that were designed to make people think in a certain way. Often this involved telling lies. Much of the propaganda tried to **justify** the hatred of the Jewish people in Germany. They were shown as weak and dishonest.

Goebbels' job was to make sure that people received only information that served the Nazi Party. He organized the burning of nearly 20,000 books written by Jews and anti-Nazi writers.

Another lie involved concentration camps. There, the Nazis killed Jews and other people they considered enemies. The Nazis wanted people to believe that the concentration camps were work camps. They said the camps provided good food, accommodation, and hospitals. However, these camps were actually created to kill Jewish people.

The Nazis produced posters that glorified leaders and the military. There were also posters that encouraged citizens to buy German goods. The aim was to make the German people feel proud of their new country and to stand behind Hitler's government. This poster reads, "The victory will be ours!"

## Ultimate Propaganda

The words over the gates of Auschwitz concentration camp in Poland read *Arbeit Macht Frei* (Work Brings Freedom). This was far from true for the people who arrived there. It is estimated that up to 1.5 million people died at Auschwitz alone. The majority were killed in rooms filled with poisonous gas.

> "**I**f you tell a lie big enough and keep repeating it, people will eventually come to believe it."
>
> —Joseph Goebbels, *German Minister of Popular Enlightenment and Propaganda*

**propaganda**
  booklets, movies, and posters put out by a government to push an idea onto society

**justify**
  prove or show as reasonable

## CASE STUDY

# Hitler Youth

One of the most important Nazi propaganda tools was an organization known as "Hitler Youth" (right). Boys had to join a junior group at a young age. They entered Hitler Youth while they were teenagers. Young girls belonged to similar groups.

Both boys and girls were taught with anti-Jewish propaganda, and they were trained to become Nazi supporters. Boys also received military training. The aim of Hitler Youth was to prepare boys to fight in the German Army. By 1945, Hitler Youth members as young as twelve were fighting in World War II.

# Jewish Persecution

## 1933-1945

Hitler's ultimate plan was to wipe out the Jewish population. This was known as the "Final Solution." The Nazi persecution of the Jews began when Hitler came to power in 1933. New laws were created to strip Jews of their rights and possessions. The Nazis destroyed Jewish synagogues, or places of worship, and businesses.

Hitler didn't stop in Germany. Between 1939 and 1941, special Nazi soldiers followed the army into conquered areas. They killed more than a million Jews in those countries, too. Millions more were forced to live with other Jews in isolation or to leave their families and work as slave laborers.

Beginning in 1942, millions of Jews were sent to concentration camps where they were killed with poisonous gas. Others were worked or starved to death. Nearly six million Jews were killed by the Nazis by the end of the war. The Nazis also killed millions of other people they considered "undesirable."

This boy has a label on his sleeve to show that he is a prisoner at a Nazi concentration camp (right).

These women and children were freed from a Nazi concentration camp by American soldiers. It is reported that between 200 and 300 prisoners a day died at their camp from starvation.

"Sometimes we slept three deep in the mud of the barracks. We were too weak to move out the dead, too weak to move ourselves, so we slept with the bodies."

—A survivor describes Gunskirchen Lager concentration camp, as recorded by American soldiers of the 71st Division

Trains carried thousands of Jews at a time to Auschwitz concentration camp. Many of them believed they were simply being moved to another part of Europe.

When prisoners arrived at a concentration camp, their belongings were taken from them. This pile of suitcases was found at Auschwitz (right).

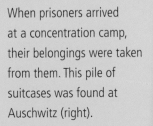

# The War Rages On

## 1940–1941

The German army used a new form of warfare known as *blitzkrieg* (BLITS KREEG), or "lightning war." World War I had been fought using **trench warfare**. Blitzkrieg focused on surprise attacks. New technology let the German Army attack from the air. They then followed up quickly with armored tanks. Germany stormed across Europe, taking control of France in June 1940.

Hitler used similar **tactics** to invade the Soviet Union. German tanks smashed through Soviet battle lines in June 1941. They took the Soviet Union by surprise. Hundreds of thousands of Soviet troops were killed or captured. It looked as if Germany would quickly win.

Fortunately for the Soviets, Hitler had not prepared his troops for a Soviet winter. The temperature dropped to a freezing 40 degrees below zero. The German soldiers were not equipped for such conditions. Their tanks and weapons broke down. The direction of World War II was turning.

A triumphant Hitler (right, center) visited Paris, France, after it was taken by German forces in June 1940. The fall of France was a great victory for Hitler.

The London Blitz destroyed the homes of many civilians (left).

London, England, was filled with smoke, fires, and wreckage following the first air raid in September 1940.

**trench warfare**
> warfare in which the opposing forces attack from trenches protected by barbed wire

**tactics**
> actions planned to win a battle

**air-raid shelters**
> structures, often underground, that protect people from bombing

# Attacks from the Air

After defeating France, Hitler wanted to invade England. However, he needed to first weaken Great Britain's Royal Air Force (RAF). The first-ever battle fought to control the air began in July 1940. It was called the Battle of Britain (above, right). By September 1940, the German Air Force—the *Luftwaffe* (LUFT VAHF uh)—mistakenly thought they had destroyed the RAF. In an attempt to force Great Britain to surrender, the Luftwaffe began bombing London.

The following air raids, known as the Blitz, caused widespread destruction. London was bombed nearly every night for eight months. Londoners took cover in **air-raid shelters** and subway tunnels. In May 1941, Germany gave up on trying to defeat Great Britain from the air.

# The Axis

Hitler's invasion of Poland in 1939 sparked the beginning of a long war. The war involved dozens of countries all over the world. Victory would come at a great price. World War II: The Axis focuses on Germany and its major Axis partners, Italy and Japan.

1.   Name the leaders of the three main Axis powers.

2.   Using World War II: The Axis as a reference, describe the way a dictatorship is run. How is this type of government different from your government?

3.   Hitler and his followers used propaganda to influence the German people. The Nazi leaders printed false statements on posters and even in newspapers.
   • Think about the last time you looked through a newspaper or watched a news program. Why do you think the German people believed what was printed in their newspapers?
   • Why do you think propaganda was an important part of Hitler's plan to win the war?

*...the victory of the democracies can only be complete with the utter defeat of the war machines of Germany and Japan.*

—General G.C. Marshall, U.S. Army Chief of Staff

# WORLD WAR II
## The Allies

When Germany invaded Poland on September 1, 1939, it confirmed what many countries feared. Adolf Hitler and his armies had begun an aggressive campaign to expand German control. The world war that followed would last six years and cost over 70 million lives.

World War II: The Allies focuses on the wartime actions of the Allies— Great Britain, France, the Soviet Union, and the United States. It shows how these countries fought to end the Axis's reign of terror.

# CONTENTS

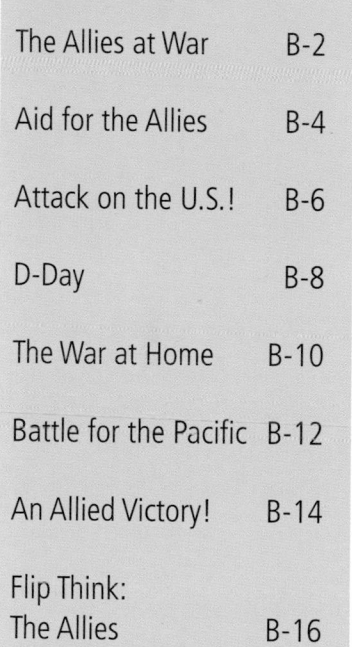

# The Allies at War

World War I (1914–1918) had been known as "The War to End All Wars." People had seen the horrors of a world war. They didn't want to believe such a tragedy could happen again. The hope for lasting peace, however, was destroyed when Germany invaded Poland on September 1, 1939.

Great Britain gave Germany two days to withdraw from Poland. The Germans refused. On September 3, 1939, Great Britain and France declared war on Germany. Most Americans did not want to get involved in another major conflict. On September 5, 1939, President Franklin D. Roosevelt declared the United States to be neutral. He did not want the U.S. military to go to Europe. However, both Roosevelt and the majority of Americans desperately wanted victory for the Allies.

The Allied invasion of German-occupied France began at Normandy, June 1944 (left).

# World War II Time Line

| | |
|---|---|
| January 30, 1933 | Adolf Hitler is appointed chancellor of Germany. |
| September 1, 1939 | Germany invades Poland—World War II begins. |
| September 3, 1939 | Britain, Australia, New Zealand, and France declare war on Germany. |
| September 5, 1939 | The United States declares its neutrality. |
| September 10, 1939 | Canada declares war on Germany. |
| May–June 1940 | French defenses collapse—British troops evacuate from Dunkirk. |
| June 10, 1940 | Italy declares war on France and Great Britain. |
| July–October 1940 | Germany attempts to defeat Great Britain's Royal Air Force in the Battle of Britain. |
| September 27, 1940 | Germany, Italy, and Japan sign a pact, forming the Axis Powers. |
| March 1941 | Congress passes the *Lend-Lease Act*. |
| June 1941 | German troops invade the Soviet Union. |
| December 7–8, 1941 | Japan bombs American military bases at Pearl Harbor in Hawaii. The United States, Britain, and Canada declare war on Japan. |
| March 1942 | The U.S. government begins moving Japanese Americans to relocation camps. |
| June 1942 | U.S. planes sink four Japanese aircraft carriers in the Battle of Midway. |
| July 1943 | The government of Italian dictator Benito Mussolini is overthrown. |
| June 6, 1944 | D-Day—Allied troops, led by General Eisenhower, land on the beaches of Normandy, France, as part of "Operation Overlord." |
| April 30, 1945 | Hitler kills himself as Soviet troops approach his quarters in Berlin. |
| May 7, 1945 | Germany surrenders in Reims, France. |
| August 6, 1945 | The United States drops an atomic bomb on Hiroshima, Japan. |
| August 9, 1945 | An atomic bomb is dropped on Nagasaki, Japan. |
| September 2, 1945 | Japan officially surrenders, ending World War II. |

"This is a sad day for all of us… There is only one thing left for me to do: That is, to devote what strength and powers I have to forwarding the victory of the cause for which we have to sacrifice so much… I trust I may live to see the day when Hitlerism has been destroyed and a liberated Europe has been re-established."

—British Prime Minister Neville Chamberlain, September 3, 1939

# Aid for the Allies

In the 1930s, the United States had passed laws about foreign wars. They stated that the United States could not aid another nation who was at war. However, Roosevelt recognized the Allies' need for ships, tanks, aircraft, and other materials. The president asked Congress to change the neutrality laws.

Congress approved military aid in 1939. They insisted on a "cash-and-carry" system. This allowed the Allies to buy weapons. However, they had to pay in cash and take care of the transportation. Roosevelt also sent 50 warships to Great Britain in exchange for naval bases in the Caribbean.

The cash-and-carry system worked well until late 1940. Then Great Britain ran out of cash to pay for weapons. Roosevelt suggested a lend-lease agreement. This would allow the United States to lend or lease equipment and weapons to any country fighting the Axis. Roosevelt argued that an Axis victory would be a threat to democracies everywhere. Congress passed the *Lend-Lease Act* in March 1941.

In 1941, the first American food ship arrived in Great Britain under the *Lend-Lease Act*. It was carrying vital food supplies for the Allies (right).

Many aircraft for both the United States Air Force and Great Britain's Royal Air Force were made in the United States.

CASE STUDY

# A Boost to the Economy

When World War II began, the United States was still suffering from the economic hardships of the Great Depression. However, the U.S. economy was significantly boosted by production for the war. There was an urgent need for large numbers of guns, jeeps, tanks, ammunition, and aircraft (above and right).

Suddenly, factories and businesses were booming. Unemployment began to fall and incomes rose. Rural areas also benefited from the war. Prices rose as U.S. farmers began supplying the Allies with food.

# Attack on the U.S.!

## 1942

U.S. involvement in World War II changed overnight. On December 7, 1941, more than 350 Japanese aircraft attacked the U.S. naval base at Pearl Harbor in Oahu, Hawaii. The Japanese hoped to cripple the American military with one blow. This would clear the way for the Japanese to expand their control of the Pacific.

The first wave of Japanese planes launched their bombs at about 7:55 A.M. (Hawaii time). Within minutes, the Japanese pilots had severely damaged the U.S.'s Pacific fleet. They destroyed 188 aircraft and sank or damaged 18 ships. There was heavy loss of life: 2,403 Americans were killed and 1,178 were wounded. Nearly half of the casualties were caused by the bombing and sinking of the ship *Arizona*.

President Roosevelt gave a famous speech the day after the attack on Pearl Harbor. Congress declared war on Japan just minutes after Roosevelt spoke. Canada and Great Britain did as well.

This photograph was taken during the attack on Pearl Harbor. "Remember Pearl Harbor!" became a rallying cry for soldiers and people at home after December 1941.

Posters and advertising campaigns were used to recruit millions of soldiers and marines for World War II. By the end of the war, about fifteen million Americans had served in the military.

READY

JOIN U.S. MARINES
LAND
SEA
AIR

APPLY, OR WRITE, TO NEAREST RECRUITING STATION

On December 8, 1941, President Roosevelt signed the declaration of war against Japan.

CASE STUDY

# Aircraft Carriers

The attack on Pearl Harbor took the United States by surprise. Japanese war planes were transported across the Pacific Ocean on large ships called aircraft carriers (above). The Japanese used the cover of darkness to get into position. The aircraft carriers quietly moved to within 200 miles north of Hawaii. They then sent their planes to drop bombs on the U.S. naval base.

# D-Day

In 1942, Great Britain and the United States began planning a large-scale invasion of France, which had been taken over by Germany. The invasion was given the codename "Operation Overlord." General Dwight D. Eisenhower was in charge. Operation Overlord was the largest naval invasion in history.

Throughout the night of June 5, 1944, thousands of ships carrying more than 175,000 Allied troops crossed the English Channel. They were headed for five landing beaches along the Normandy coast. **Minesweepers** had gone first to clear the water of mines, or floating bombs. Thousands of **paratroopers** had been dropped behind enemy lines. Their job was to take control of key bridges and railroad tracks.

At dawn on June 6, 1944, battleships opened fire on the beaches. Allied troops then stormed onto the shore. After fierce fighting, all five beaches were taken by Allied forces. The attack came to be known as D-Day.

Allied troops poured into France. By the end of June, about a million soldiers were advancing toward key locations. Operation Overlord ended when the **Free French Forces** and American troops **liberated** Paris on August 25.

The German army was expecting an attack on France's north coast. The Germans thought the Allies would land near Calais. General Eisenhower took Hitler by surprise when he had the Allied troops land in Normandy (right).

# Normandy Landing: The Largest Naval Invasion in History

**ENGLAND**

Portsmouth
Southampton
Portland
Dartmouth
Shoreham-by-Sea
Calais
Strait of Dover
English Channel
Dieppe
**FRANCE**
Caen
**NORMANDY**

**Key**
- American forces
- British forces
- Canadian forces

**minesweepers**
  warships made to find and destroy explosives in the water

**paratroopers**
  soldiers trained in using parachutes

**Free French Forces**
  French soldiers who continued to fight for the Allies after France surrendered to Germany

**liberated**
  set free from the enemy

**coordinate**
  to arrange; to organize

CASE STUDY

# Plans for D-Day

General Dwight D. Eisenhower was the commander of the Allied Forces in Europe (right). It was his responsibility to organize Operation Overlord. He had to **coordinate** the armies and navies of the United States, Great Britain, and Canada.

He also had to coordinate the invasion to tie in with low tides, calm seas, and clear weather conditions. Otherwise, the invasion could be ruined. The Allies rehearsed their plan of attack over and over. Their timing had to be exact. They were determined to succeed, and they did.

# The War at Home

## 1940–1945

All U.S. citizens were affected by the war. Life changed dramatically, even for people at home. Everyone needed to make sacrifices for the war effort. **Restrictions** were placed on items needed by the armed forces. These items included canned foods and tires. The U.S. government issued **ration stamps**. The stamps limited purchases of certain supplies that were needed overseas. These included gasoline, coffee, meat, and shoes.

People were encouraged to plant vegetable gardens. These were known as "Victory Gardens." This guaranteed there was enough food for people at home as well as for the troops fighting overseas. Victory Gardens were planted in window boxes, backyards, vacant lots, parks, and baseball fields. Sometimes scarecrows were used to protect the vegetables from birds. Some of the Victory Garden scarecrows were created to look like Axis dictators.

Money was also needed to pay for the war. The U.S. government increased taxes. They also sold **war bonds** to the public. This was a way that average Americans could loan money to the government for the war. Americans bought billions of dollars worth of war bonds.

The first nonfood item to be rationed was rubber. President Roosevelt asked people to help the war effort by donating scrap rubber to be recycled. Tires, rubber raincoats, garden hoses, rubber shoes, and bathing caps were all collected and recycled.

Mary Pickford was a famous movie star. She and other celebrities traveled the country to encourage people to buy war bonds.

**restrictions**
limits or rules placed on something

**ration stamps**
government-issued coupons that were needed to get certain goods

**war bonds**
government-issued investments or savings

FOR EVERY FIGHTER A WOMAN WORKER. Y.W.C.A.

BACK OUR SECOND LINE OF DEFENSE
UNITED WAR WORK CAMPAIGN

CASE STUDY

# Women Working for War

Many jobs needed to be filled when millions of men left for the war. Wartime industry also created many new jobs. The U.S. government encouraged women to fill jobs in factories and offices (right).

About 300,000 women also worked in the armed forces. Some women worked as nurses. Others flew planes from factories to military units. World War II provided many new opportunities for women.

# Battle for the Pacific

## 1942–1945

After the bombing of Pearl Harbor, Japan quickly took control of U.S. territories in the Pacific Ocean. Many Americans thought that the West Coast might be a Japanese target, too.

The Allies knew they had to stop Japan's advance. Fortunately, they had a top-secret weapon. Allied code breakers had cracked Japan's secret messages. The U.S. Navy now had **access** to the battle plans of the Japanese. In May 1942, the Allies attacked the Japanese in the Battle of the Coral Sea off the northeast coast of Australia. The Allies stopped Japan from taking a major port. The tide had turned against Japan.

Weeks later, the U.S. Navy again **intercepted** top-secret information. They used this information to cripple the Japanese in the Battle of Midway. In 1943, the Allies began targeting Japanese strongholds.

By 1945, the United States and Japan were fighting over the Japanese islands Iwo Jima (EE woh JEE mah) and Okinawa (oh KUH NOW wuh). Gaining control of at least one of these islands was essential for the United States. They needed to secure a base for short-range fighter planes.

The Japanese fought a fierce battle. About 25,000 U.S. troops were killed. The United States captured Iwo Jima on March 6.

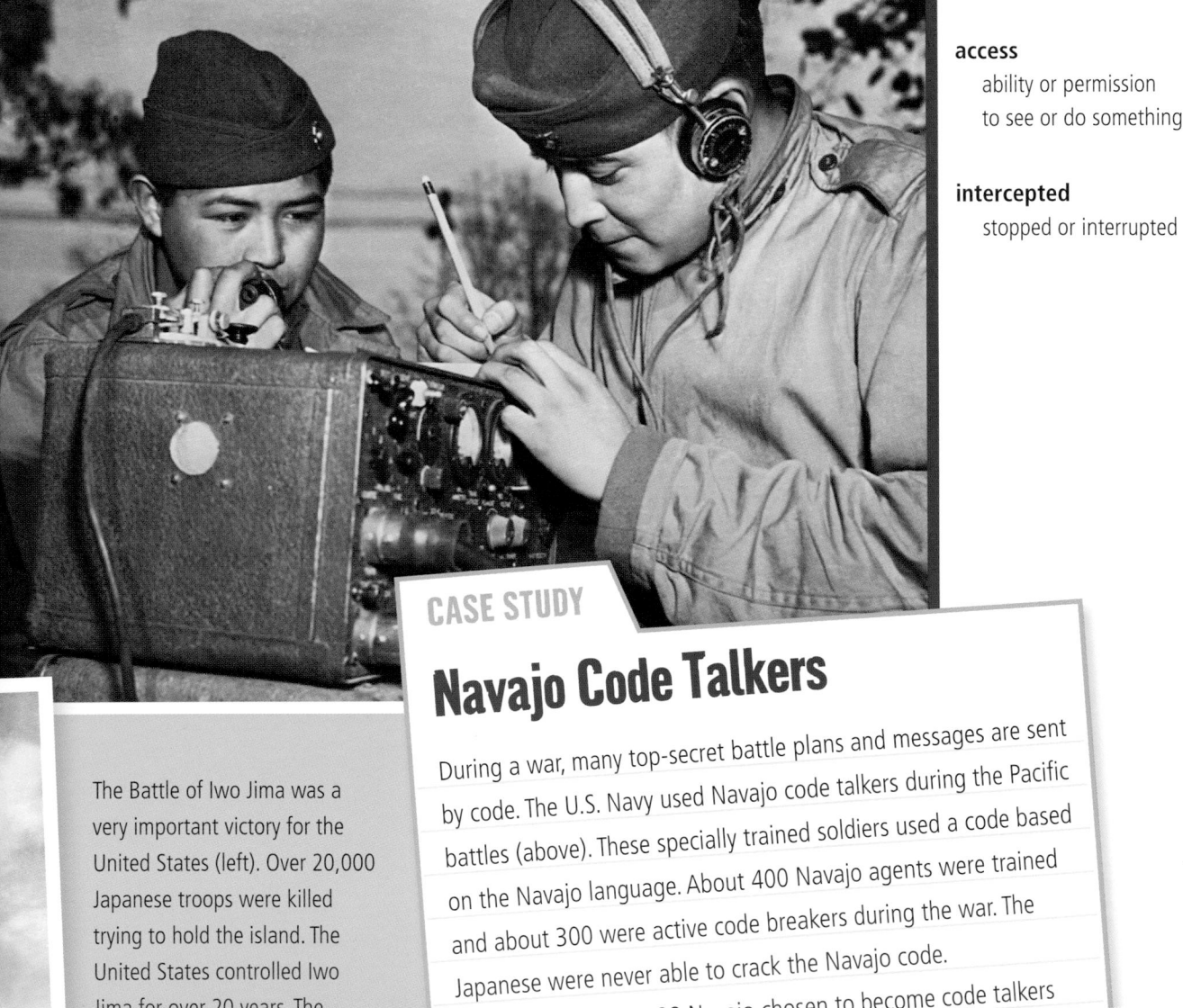

The Battle of Iwo Jima was a very important victory for the United States (left). Over 20,000 Japanese troops were killed trying to hold the island. The United States controlled Iwo Jima for over 20 years. The island was returned to Japan in 1968.

**CASE STUDY**

# Navajo Code Talkers

During a war, many top-secret battle plans and messages are sent by code. The U.S. Navy used Navajo code talkers during the Pacific battles (above). These specially trained soldiers used a code based on the Navajo language. About 400 Navajo agents were trained and about 300 were active code breakers during the war. The Japanese were never able to crack the Navajo code.

In 2001, the first 29 Navajo chosen to become code talkers received Congressional Gold Medals in appreciation of their services to the United States. The remaining code talkers were awarded silver medals.

# An Allied Victory!

## 1945

The Allies began their final battle against Germany in early 1945. Major German cities were bombed repeatedly, causing great damage. British and Canadian troops swept into Germany through the Netherlands. American and French troops headed toward central Germany. Soviet troops occupied most of Eastern Europe. As the Allies advanced, they saw the suffering that took place under Hitler's rule.

An Allied victory looked certain, but Hitler ordered his troops to fight on. When Soviet troops began to surround Germany's capital city of Berlin, Hitler committed suicide. Germany surrendered on May 7, 1945. The following day, May 8, was declared V-E Day—Victory in Europe Day. The war in Europe was over.

In the Pacific, however, Japan continued its fight. The Allies warned Japan to surrender or face total disaster. Japan's leaders ignored the warning. In early August, new U.S. President Harry S. Truman ordered the military to drop weapons called atomic bombs on two Japanese cities. The cities were **demolished**. Japan finally surrendered on September 2. World War II was over.

Japan officially surrendered aboard the U.S. battleship *Missouri* (right), which was at anchor in Tokyo Bay. Representatives of all the Allied nations were there to watch the ceremonies.

The atomic bombs dropped on Hiroshima and Nagasaki caused massive destruction. Those two bombs were the first and last such weapons used in war.

**demolished**
destroyed

**radiation poisoning**
illness caused by exposure to atomic energy

CASE STUDY

# The Atomic Bomb

In 1939, German-born scientist Albert Einstein wrote a letter to President Roosevelt. Einstein explained that Germany might be making a superbomb. The president was concerned that Hitler might win the war with such a weapon. The United States set up a top-secret program to develop its own atomic bomb.

On August 6, 1945, the United States dropped an atomic bomb on the Japanese city of Hiroshima. Between 70,000 and 80,000 people died from the blast. Japan still refused to surrender. On August 9, another atomic bomb was dropped on the city of Nagasaki, killing about 40,000 people. Thousands more in both cities died later from injuries or **radiation poisoning**. The atomic bombs caused great destruction, but they forced the Japanese emperor to surrender.

# The Allies

Hitler's invasion of Poland in 1939 sparked the beginning of a long war. The war involved dozens of countries all over the world. Victory would come at a great price. World War II: The Allies focuses on the wartime actions of the United States and its major allies—Great Britain, France, and the Soviet Union.

1.  What was the name of the agreement that enabled the United States to provide equipment and weapons to any country fighting the Axis?

2.  Using World War II: The Allies as a reference, find the date Japan attacked Pearl Harbor. How did the United States respond?

3.  When Japan attacked Pearl Harbor, the United States decided to join the Allied Powers in the war. Before the attack, though, the United States had wanted to be a neutral nation.
    - Think about a time when someone you know was mistreated. How did that make you feel? How did you respond?
    - Why do you think the U.S. Congress declared war on all the Axis nations after Japan attacked Pearl Harbor?